OUR SOLAR SYSTEM

Space Exploration

BY DANA MEACHEN RAU

Content Adviser: Dr. Stanley P. Jones, Assistant Director, Washington, D.C., Operations, NASA Classroom of the Future

Science Adviser: Terrence E. Young Jr., M.Ed., M.L.S., Jefferson Parish (La.) Public Schools

Reading Adviser: Dr. Linda D. Labbo, Department of Reading Education, College of Education, The University of Georgia

COMPASS POINT BOOKS
MINNEAPOLIS, MINNESOTA

Compass Point Books
3109 West 50th Street, #115
Minneapolis, MN 55410

Visit Compass Point Books on the Internet at *www.compasspointbooks.com*
or e-mail your request to *custserv@compasspointbooks.com*

Photographs ©: PhotoDisc, cover, 1, 5, 14, 16, 21, 22–23; DigitalVision, 3, 17, 19, 20 (all); Bettmann/Corbis, 4 (all), 7, 8 (bottom), 9 (all), 12; Myron Jay Dorf/Corbis, 6; Gianni Dagli Orti/Corbis, 8 (top); Roger Ressmeyer/Corbis, 10–11, 13 (bottom); Archivo Iconografico, S.A./Corbis, 13 (top); NASA photo courtesy of Space Images, 15, 18; Todd Boroson (NOAO)/AURA/NOAO/NSF, 24–25.

Editors: E. Russell Primm, Emily J. Dolbear, and Catherine Neitge
Photo Researchers: Svetlana Zhurkina and Marcie Spence
Photo Selector: Linda S. Koutris
Designer: The Design Lab
Illustrator: Graphicstock

Library of Congress Cataloging-in-Publication Data
Rau, Dana Meachen, 1971–
   Space exploration / by Dana Rau.
      p. cm.— (Our solar system)
Includes bibliographical references and index.
Contents: A huge universe to explore—Looking to the sky—Telescopes: important tools—Unmanned missions—Manned missions—The future of space exploration.
   ISBN 0-7565-0439-2 (hardcover)
   1. Outer space—Exploration—Juvenile literature. [1. Outer space—Exploration. 2. Space flight.] I. Title.
   QB500.262 .R38 2003
   919.904—dc21   2002009939

Table of Contents

NOTE: In this book, words that are defined in the glossary are in **bold** the first time they appear in the text.

A Huge Universe to Explore

Earth is a large place. Long ago, people didn't know a lot about Earth. They set out to explore it. They walked over the land. They sailed across the oceans. Today, there are still parts of Earth left to explore.

Earth is small compared to the universe. Earth is one of nine planets that travel around the Sun, or revolve, in paths

Lewis and Clark (above) and Henry Hudson (below) explored North America when little was known about it. Today there are still parts of Earth that have yet to be explored.

Nine planets orbit the Sun, which is only one of several billion stars in the Milky Way galaxy.

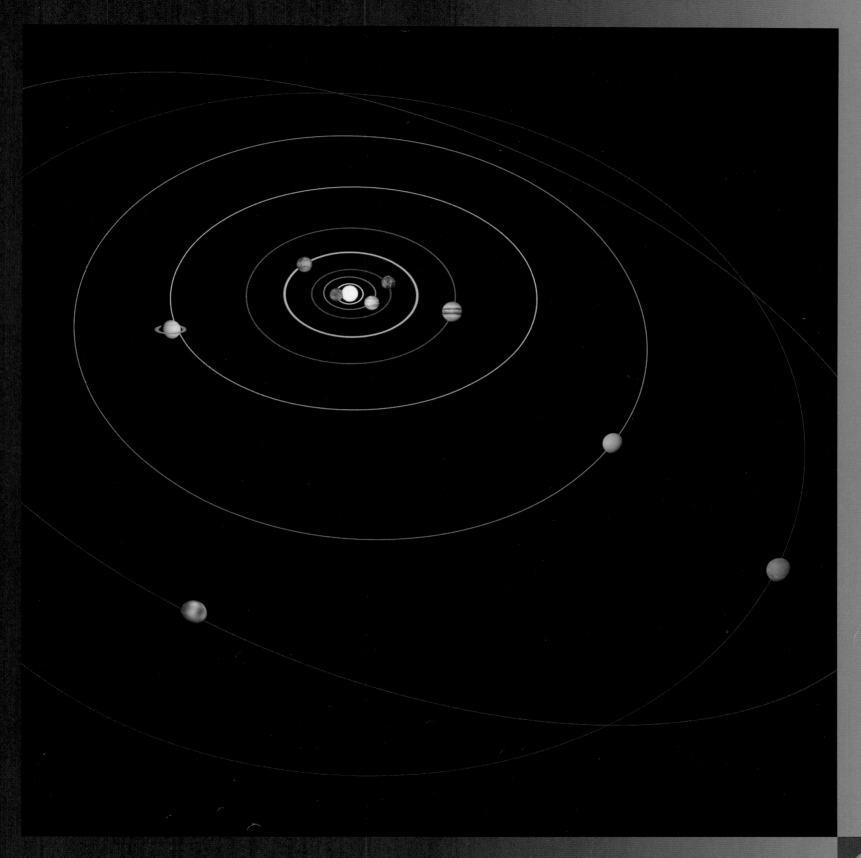

called orbits. The Sun and the planets are part of the **solar system**. The Sun is one of billions of stars in the Milky Way **galaxy**. The Milky Way galaxy is one of hundreds of billions of galaxies in the universe. The universe is a very big place!

People on Earth are curious about the universe. They want to find out how the solar system formed. They want to know if there is any life on other planets. They also want to know how our solar system, and the rest of the universe, may change in the future.

The Milky Way is one of hundreds of ▼ billions of galaxies in the universe.

Looking to the Sky

The ancient Greeks studied the night sky.

The earliest people on Earth looked up to the sky and wondered about the Sun, Moon, stars, and planets. They used the cycles of the Sun and Moon to divide time into hours, days, months, and years. People who lived in Egypt and Mesopotamia long ago used the Sun and Moon to create their calendars. Some of these calendars were made four thousand years ago.

More than two thousand years ago, **astronomers** figured

out the correct size of the Sun and the Moon. In the year 140, the Greek astronomer Ptolemy had the idea that the Sun and the other planets orbited Earth. Then, in the 1500s, the Polish astronomer Nicolaus Copernicus had a different idea. He believed that the Sun is the center of the solar system and the planets orbit around the Sun.

Over time, astronomers have made important discoveries about space. In the 1600s, the Italian astronomer Galileo Galilei (1564–1642) discovered moons around Jupiter

Ptolemy (above), who lived in the second century, and Copernicus (1473–1543) had different ideas about the Sun.

and many other facts about the solar system. In the 1700s, the English astronomer Edmond Halley made exciting discoveries about **comets**. In the twentieth century, Carl Sagan led the search for life beyond Earth. U.S. astronomer Edwin Hubble (1889–1953) discovered that there are many galaxies besides the Milky Way. These galaxies are always moving away from each other. This means that the universe is getting bigger all the time.

◀ *Edmond Halley (1656–1742) (above) made important discoveries about comets. Carl Sagan (1934–1996) believed life might exist on other planets.*

Telescopes: Important Tools

One of the most important tools astronomers use is the telescope. It makes objects in space look larger. This way, objects in space can be studied more closely.

The first telescope was invented by a Dutch optician named Hans Lippershey in 1608. An optician is someone who works with pieces of glass called lenses. Lippershey was holding two lenses together. He noticed that the object he saw through them

Telescopes help astronomers study the solar system. ▶

looked larger than it did without the lenses. In 1609, Galileo was the first person to use a telescope to look at objects in the sky.

In 1668, an Englishman named Sir Isaac Newton invented another type of telescope. It used mirrors instead of lenses.

Most astronomers today use this kind of telescope. Objects in the sky can be seen more clearly.

Even with a telescope, however, it is hard to get a clear view. Earth is surrounded by a layer of gas. This layer is called its

Hans Lippershey invented the ▼
first telescope in 1608.

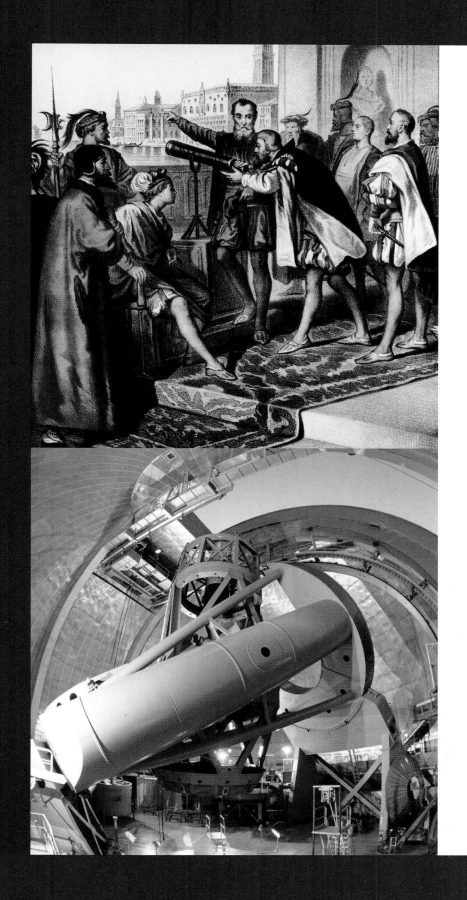

atmosphere. The atmosphere sometimes makes our view of outer space look fuzzy. Astronomers wanted to be able to look at space without having to look through the atmosphere. In 1990, the Hubble Space Telescope (HST) was sent into space to orbit Earth. The HST is able to get views of objects in space that can't be seen from Earth. The HST has taken thousands of pictures. They show stars being formed and even a comet crashing into the planet Jupiter.

◀ *A telescope used long ago by the astronomer Galileo (above), and a modern telescope at Mount Palomar Observatory in California*

Unmanned Missions

✦ Astronomers have explored space by looking at it from Earth. They have also explored space by sending spacecraft to look at planets, the Sun, and other objects more closely.

A mission takes place when a spacecraft is sent into space. The National Aeronautics and Space Administration (NASA) is the part of the U.S. government in charge of space missions. There are two types of

NASA sends many missions into space. ▶

missions. One type is called manned. The other type is called unmanned. Manned missions have astronauts traveling inside the spacecraft. Unmanned missions do not have astronauts on board. The spacecraft collects information and takes pictures. Unmanned missions can go to places that are not safe for people to go.

There are many types of unmanned missions. Some spacecraft fly by planets and collect information as they go past. Two of the most successful flyby missions were of the spacecraft *Voyager 1* and *Voyager 2.* They studied four of the planets farthest from the Sun. Those planets are Jupiter, Saturn, Uranus, and Neptune. Other spacecraft orbit planets. As a spacecraft orbits, it takes pictures and collects information. An **orbiter** spends much more time near the planet than

▲ Voyager 1 *was part of a flyby mission.*

a flyby spacecraft, so it can give astronomers more information. It can make maps of the surface of the planet. Astronomers can see changes on the surface because the orbiter passes the same spot more than once. *Galileo* is an orbiter that has been orbiting Jupiter since 1995. It has given astronomers an amazing amount of information about Jupiter and its many moons.

Sometimes an orbiter also carries a probe. This is a smaller spacecraft that is dropped toward a planet's

Galileo *continues to collect a great* ▶
deal of information about Jupiter.

surface. On its way down, it collects information. A probe called *Huygens* is on its way to Saturn. When it arrives in 2004, it will drop toward Titan, one of Saturn's moons. Titan is the only moon with an atmosphere like a planet. As *Huygens* falls, it will tell us more about the atmosphere.

Some spacecraft are **landers**. The *Mars Pathfinder* lander had an exciting mission. It landed on Mars in July 1997. It studied Mars's surface for three months. It also had a rover, named *Sojourner,* on board. A rover is a vehicle that astronomers

◀ *The probe* Huygens *will drop toward Titan in 2004.*

control from Earth. *Sojourner* drove along the surface of Mars. More rovers are being sent to Mars to look for clues that water was once present. The new rovers weigh 400 pounds (182 kilograms) each and are much bigger than *Sojourner.*

Back on Earth, astronomers track the missions closely. Some missions are short. Others go on for many years. Unmanned spacecraft gather information until they stop working or until they are too far away from Earth to send back information.

The Sojourner *rover during its 1997 mission to Mars* ▶

Manned Missions

★ Another way to explore space is to send manned missions. So far, the only object in the solar system that has been visited by humans is the Moon. In the 1960s, NASA trained its astronauts to travel into space. It built spacecraft designed to land and take off from the Moon's surface. In 1969, NASA sent three astronauts on a mission to the Moon in the *Apollo 11* spacecraft. Two of the astronauts, Neil Armstrong and Edwin "Buzz" Aldrin, became the first

◀ *Edwin "Buzz" Aldrin during his 1969 trip to the Moon*

men to walk on the Moon. They collected Moon rocks and brought them back to Earth. More astronauts were sent in other Apollo missions. In all, twelve men have walked on the Moon.

During the Apollo missions, astronauts returned to Earth by splashing down their spacecraft into the ocean. Boats waiting for them brought them safely home. NASA wanted to find a way to create a spacecraft that could be used over and over again. It built the space shuttle. *Columbia* was the world's first space

When Neil Armstrong made this footprint ▶ on the Moon in 1969 (above), space shuttles like the one shown were still years away.

shuttle. Its first mission began on April 12, 1981. Its twenty-eighth mission ended in tragedy on February 1, 2003.

Something went terribly wrong on *Columbia's* return to Earth. It broke apart on reentry into Earth's atmosphere, killing the seven astronauts on board.

Columbia was one of four space shuttles, where astronauts performed experiments and did many other jobs. The shuttle crews helped fix **satellites** and repaired the Hubble Space Telescope. Following the accident, NASA is studying the future of the space shuttle program.

◀ *Astronauts have many jobs to do in space.*

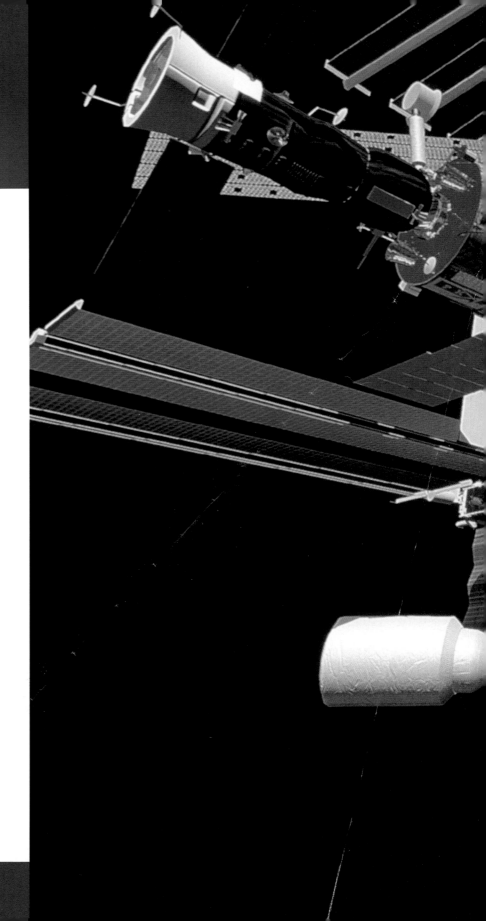

The Future of Space Exploration

✦ The astronauts of space shuttle missions have been working on a new and exciting way to explore space. They are building a large space station that orbits Earth. It is called the International Space Station. When it is finished, it will be a place where astronauts can live and work for three to six months.

In the International Space Station, the astronauts will perform many experiments.

Space stations will allow astronauts a ▶ longer and more comfortable stay in space.

They will find out if longer missions to other planets, such as Mars, can take place. They will be able to study space better from there than from Earth.

There is so much to discover about the universe. Astronomers have already found planets orbiting other stars, much like in our own solar system. There may be another planet like Earth somewhere in the universe.

There are many ways for astronomers to explore space. They are always look-

Exploring space will tell us more ▶
about our solar system and other
galaxies yet to be studied.

ing for new ways as well. Just like people did before the inventions of spacecraft and telescopes, humans will always look into the sky and wonder about the universe.

People will always be hopeful, as well. Sally Ride, the first U.S. woman in space, said that despite the *Columbia* tragedy, the space program will go on. "It will continue and it will be better than it is today," she said. "We'll pick up the torch the astronauts carried and carry it forward."

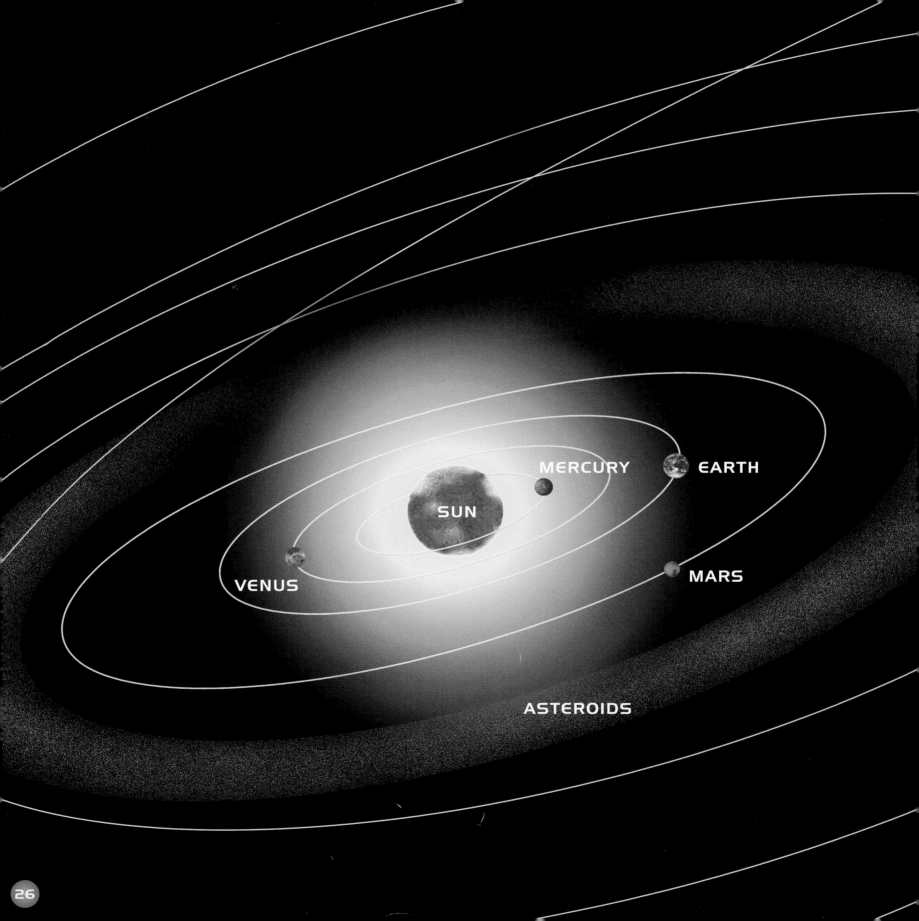

JUPITER

URANUS

SATURN

NEPTUNE

PLUTO

27

Glossary

astronomers—people who study space

comets—pieces of ice and rock that have long tails of dust and orbit the Sun

galaxy—a very large group of stars

landers—parts of spacecraft that land on a planet's surface

orbiter—a spacecraft that orbits a planet or other space object

satellites—objects that orbit a planet; some satellites that orbit Earth study land and weather or help with communication

solar system—a group of objects in space including the Sun, planets, moons, asteroids, comets, and meteoroids

Did You Know?

- Some spacecraft return samples to Earth. Many Moon rocks were brought back to Earth during the *Apollo* missions. *Stardust* is currently on its way to a comet to bring back pieces for scientists to study.

- Spacecraft have been sent to study all of the planets in the solar system except Pluto. A mission to that planet is being planned.

- Taking the Hubble Space Telescope into space was one of the most exciting missions of the space shuttle. It was released into orbit by the space shuttle *Discovery* in 1990.

- In the 1960s, the United States and the Soviet Union (now Russia) competed with each other to be the first to put a man on the Moon. The United States won the "space race" when Americans walked on the Moon on July 20, 1969.

- Manned missions are watched from Earth by Mission Control in Houston, Texas. The people of Mission Control keep close watch on the astronauts and make sure everything is running smoothly.

- On the space shuttle, astronauts are weightless. That means they float around the spacecraft. They have to tie themselves down to sleep.

- The first space station was the *Salyut*. It was launched by the Soviet Union in 1971. The U.S. space station *Skylab* was launched in 1973. The Russian space station *Mir* was launched in 1986. It stayed in space for about fifteen years.

Want to Know More?

AT THE LIBRARY

Becklake, Sue. *All About Space.* New York: Scholastic Reference, 1998.

Fowler, Allan. *The Sun's Family of Planets.* Chicago: Childrens Press, 1993.

Rau, Dana Meachen. *The Solar System.* Minneapolis: Compass Point Books, 2000.

Scott, Elaine. *Close Encounters: Exploring the Universe with the Hubble Space Telescope.*
 New York: Hyperion Books for Children, 1998.

ON THE WEB

Exploring the Planets: Tools of Exploration

http://www.nasm.edu/ceps/etp/tools/etptools.html

For detailed information about all the ways astronomers explore space

NASA Human Spaceflight

http://spaceflight.nasa.gov/

For information about shuttle missions, the International Space Station, and the history of space flight

Solar System Exploration

http://sse.jpl.nasa.gov/

For everything about space exploration—from its history, to a list of all missions, to plans for the future

Solar Views: History of Space Exploration

http://www.solarviews.com/eng/history.htm

For information about the many missions sent into space

Space Kids

http://spacekids.hq.nasa.gov

NASA's space science site designed just for kids

Space.com

http://www.space.com

For the latest news about everything to do with space

Windows to the Universe

http://www.windows.ucar.edu

For information about all types of space subjects, from the earliest ideas about space, to important astronomers, to details about the many objects in the solar system

THROUGH THE MAIL

Goddard Space Flight Center
Code 130, Public Affairs Office
Greenbelt, MD 20771
To learn more about space exploration

Jet Propulsion Laboratory
Public Services Office Mail Stop 186-113
4800 Oak Grove Drive
Pasadena, CA 91109
818/354-9314
To learn more about the spacecraft
missions

Lunar and Planetary Institute
3600 Bay Area Boulevard
Houston, TX 77058
To learn more about the solar system

Space Science Division
NASA Ames Research Center
Moffet Field, CA 94035
To learn more about solar
system exploration

Mount Wilson Institute
Hale Solar Laboratory
P.O. Box 60947
Pasadena, CA 91116
626/793-3100
To learn more about the observatory
where Edwin Hubble did his research
about the universe

ON THE ROAD

**Adler Planetarium and
Astronomy Museum**
1300 S. Lake Shore Drive
Chicago, IL 60605-2403
312/922-STAR
To visit the oldest planetarium in
the Western Hemisphere

***Exploring the Planets* and
*Where Next, Columbus?***
National Air and Space Museum
7th and Independence Avenue, S.W.
Washington, DC 20560
202/357-2700
To learn more about the solar system and
space exploration at this museum exhibit

**Rose Center for Earth and
Space/Hayden Planetarium**
Central Park West at 79th Street
New York, NY 10024-5192
212/769-5100
To visit this new planetarium and learn
more about the solar system

UCO/Lick Observatory
University of California
Santa Cruz, CA 95064
408/274-5061
To see the telescope that was used to
discover the first planets outside of our
solar system

Index

◀ **About the Author:** *Dana Meachen Rau loves to study space. Her office walls are covered with pictures of planets, astronauts, and spacecraft. She also likes to look up at the sky with her telescope and write poems about what she sees. Ms. Rau is the author of more than seventy-five books for children, including nonfiction, biographies, storybooks, and early readers. She lives in Burlington, Connecticut, with her husband, Chris, and children, Charlie and Allison.*